Protein is the most valuable vital nutrient in your diet. Your body is made up of protein—hopefully it isn't just made of fat. Every day you lose a little of this power fuel and every day you must replenish it. Because many protein sources in our diets also include fat, and fat hinders protein digestion, I recommend eating protein with little or no fat, such as in the form of tender fish, lean poultry, cottage cheese, yogurt, and legumes. But because these foods are not always available, I suggest you also use a high-quality protein powder, preferably in combination with fruit or vegetables as found in these fitness drinks.

Put in a power week with our fitness drinks. You'll lose a pound a day while gaining vitality and well-being. Here's to your health!

Dr. Ulrich Strunz

D0817378

Protein:

Keeps body, mind, and spirit fit

The Power Fuel

Every aspect of our bodies, including both our physical and our mental health, is determined by protein. Nutrients such as vitamins, trace elements, minerals, fatty acids, and carbohydrates are merely auxiliary materials that help activate the protein. From the 24 amino acids that you must consume every day, your body assembles around 50,000 different proteins: Your immune system, your muscles, your hormones, your emotions, your life.

PROTEIN DEFICIENCY DESPITE EXCESS

Protein is abundantly present in our normal diet. Not only is it contained in fish, lean meat, poultry, low-fat cheese and milk products, but also in vegetables, whole grains, and legumes. Nevertheless, many people suffer from a protein deficiency. They utilize protein badly. If you don't absorb enough nutrients, if you eat too much fat or too much sugar, protein never reaches its place of effectiveness, the 70 billion cells in your body. Your mind slows down and your immune system weakens, your body stores globs of fat, your muscles dwindle, your skin ages, and your organs lose their capacity to perform.

The Most Valuable Ingredient

If you weigh 150 pounds, 30 of those pounds are pure protein, including your hair, bones and joints, enzymes and hormones, muscles, immune system, and blood. Protein is truly the most valuable ingredient in your food, the building blocks from which your life, moods, and energy are constructed. What you eat each day must supply your body with a booster shot of protein that it can use to produce hormones, keep your immune system up and running, build up muscles, and repair cells. But whether the protein actually reaches its place of effectiveness, the cells, can be seen only by looking at your blood. The average person's blood protein level is low, resulting in fragile bones, weak muscles, a lack of red, oxygen-carrying blood cells, a listless immune system, and an unsteady psyche. People with a high blood protein level are life's winners. Nothing keeps them down.

How Much Protein Do You Have In Your Blood?

A low protein content indicates that your body is running on half steam. With a blood protein level of:

* 8 g/dl you feel good and are active;
* 7 g/dl you feel pretty good;
* 6 g/dl you're tired and without energy.

Ask your doctor to tell you your level.

Fill Up Your Protein Tank

When you have a lot of protein in your blood, you become more alert, you have better concentration, and you're happier. So raise your protein level to the top of the normal range. To do this, you'll have to fill your body up with protein over the course of several weeks. Too much all at once won't help you. Your body eliminates the surplus, causing damage to your kidneys. So give your body only a small dose of extra protein each day, just enough to refill its empty stores. The ideal is one serving of protein every four hours because it takes the protein four hours to pass through your kidneys and exit your body. It's a somewhat tedious process but just consider the rewards: Vitality, lust for life, and energy!

How Much Protein Does a Person Need?

At least 20 percent of the calories you consume in a day should be in the form of protein. It is estimated that you need about 0.8 grams of protein per 2 pounds of body weight. Therefore a person weighing 130 pounds has a minimum requirement of 48 grams. However, athletes, people with high-stress jobs, and people with an overall low blood protein level need more protein—up to twice as much.

Magic

Create energy and good moods

Amino Acids

There are ten amino acids that are especially important to your body—your body can't produce these amino acids on its own or can produce only to a limited extent. If you don't get them from your diet, the other amino acids are also rendered useless, like a house missing its beams.

LEUCINE KEEPS YOU FIT

Leucine is an important building block in blood protein and tissues. This amino acid is essential for muscular stamina and physical performance. If you don't have enough, your entire body is weakened.

ISOLEUCINE COMBATS STRESS

Isoleucine is essential for muscular stamina and works as a brain-activating amino acid. This amino acid mainly produces neurotransmitters (chemicals that transmit messages for the brain) that protect you against stress.

LYSINE KEEPS YOU YOUNG

As a component of collagen, lysine keeps your skin firm and protects your arteries from sclerosis. As a building block of enzymes, lysine stimulates the growth hormone (the physiological fountain of youth), which builds up muscle and burns off fat. Without lysine, there are no enzymes to fight cancer cells. Lysine is also a component of carnitine, the nutrient that channels fat to the cells, thus making fat combustion possible. Lysine strengthens your resistance to viruses and can help those suffering from a lack of drive or difficulty concentrating.

METHIONINE—METABOLISM'S JACK OF ALL TRADES

Methionine is the starting point for all protein synthesis. This amino acid is a component of carnitine, which transports fat to the cells where it is combusted. Methionine is important for the defense function (phagocytic ability) of the killer cells in the blood. It also protects our body's detoxifier, the liver.

THREONINE PERKS UP WEARY SOULS

Threonine is the key substance in the production of the endothelial relaxing factor, meaning that it is essential for dilating the blood vessels and, thus, for the flow of blood through the body, heart, and brain. A deficiency often results in constricted blood vessels, fatigue, and even heart trouble.

Phenylalanine Lifts Spirits and Stops Hunger

This amino acid is a basic material for mood elevating hormones such as norepinephrine, ACTH, dopamine, and endorphins. Phenylalanine helps relieve depression and build self-esteem. It's also used as a pain remedy for arthritis, rheumatism, and muscular pain. In the intestines, phenylalanine helps regulate cholecystokinin, the hormone that signals the brain when you're full.

Tryptophan Relaxes

The body uses tryptophan to produce melatonin, the fountain-of-youth hormone, as well as serotonin, the chief hormone for inner peace, equanimity, and happiness. When you're under stress, anxious or having difficulty sleeping, or if you want to quit smoking, take an extra helping of tryptophan. A deficiency can result in depression and even psychoses.

Valine Peps Up Nerves and Your Immune System

Valine promotes the healthy functioning of your nervous system and aids in the production of hemoglobin, the red blood pigment that transports revitalizing oxygen to all your cells. Valine is also important for building up an active immune system.

Histidine Puts the Wind in Your Sails

Histidine is also required for producing the oxygen-carrying red hemoglobin. In other words, the more histidine you have, the better you perform, both physically and mentally. Histidine regulates cell growth and regeneration. The cells' tiny power plants, the mitochondria, require this amino acid for transporting oxygen and, therefore, for producing power.

Taurine Keeps You Thin

This protein material is important for overeaters and food lovers because taurine increases fat combustion by a factor of four. And taurine detoxifies the liver whenever it suffers a toxic overload (such as from alcohol). This amino acid also blocks the unpleasant effects of caffeine by slowing down your pulse.

Eat Protein with
Stay fit and trim
Little or No Fat

Is too much protein a bad thing? Certainly "too much" of anything is bad, even too much oxygen. We can't live without oxygen, but when there's too much it becomes toxic. The question is, how much is too much? Your body is made up of about 30 pounds of protein. Every day you lose a handful of it, from 2 to 4 ounces, and every day you have to replenish it.

Most people have a low protein level even when they eat a huge amount of protein, usually in the form of meat. The problem is that the protein on your plate never reaches the places where you need it most, the places in your body where the tiny protein building blocks, the amino acids, work to raise your spirits, repair cells, mobilize your immune system, build up your muscles, and get your power hormones moving. And why doesn't it reach its destination? First of all, because you lack the vital nutrients required for digesting protein. Nutritious protein is lying inert in your intestines, bloating you, and causing allergies.

Secondly, because you eat protein with fat. If you really want to fill up your tank with protein power, you need to eat protein on its own, without the fat. Fat prevents the valuable amino acids from participating in metabolism, starting in your intestines. Fat hinders peristalsis, the movement of the intestines. It takes only a minimal amount of fat to delay the absorption of protein into the bloodstream by several hours. The amino acids barely trickle into your bloodstream and can't reach their place of effectiveness fast enough or in large enough quantities to do you any good. Unless the correct amount of protein is made available all at once, your body can never activate sufficient quantities of hormones and neurotransmitters, elevate your brain to a state of euphoria, render your thoughts crystal-clear, fill you full of self-confidence, or help you achieve your highest level of performance. Where can you find protein with little or no fat? Valuable sources include tender fish, lean poultry, cottage cheese, yogurt, and other low-fat dairy products, as well as legumes. But since you can't have a plateful of these foods every four hours, I suggest that you also use a high-quality protein powder, preferably in combination with fruit or vegetables. Fruits and vegetables provide the nutrients you need to transport the protein to the 70 billion cells in your body, making you thin and happy, healthy and fit, stress-proof and creative, youthful and beautiful.

PROTEIN POWDER FROM THE STORE

Because protein is almost always combined with fat, you can seldom consume enough protein to fill up your empty stores without simultaneously broadening your hips. So go to the health food store and buy protein without fat. A good protein powder is an excellent means of raising your blood protein level. After only a few days you will see—or rather feel—that you have more power, your thoughts are clearer, and your mood simply couldn't be better.

Important: If you fill up your tank with protein powder, you also need to drink a lot of liquid—at least three quarts a day.

A GOOD POWDER

A protein powder from the health food store is "good" if it contains 60 percent animal protein (usually from egg whites and milk) and 40 percent plant protein (frequently soy). You'll know it's high-quality if it says "biological value over 100" on the label. In addition, an extra serving of carnitine in the protein powder helps you lose weight. Added vitamins and minerals will ensure an efficient protein metabolism and help fill up empty vital nutrient tanks.

PROTEIN POWDER AS A FITNESS DRINK

As an accompaniment to a healthy low-sugar, low-fat diet, consuming one or two of our fitness drinks every day will help you fill up your empty tanks.

Naturally, you can also simply dissolve the powder in water or low-fat milk. But then make sure you also eat some fruit or vegetables because these foods contain the active ingredients that render the protein biologically active in your body. But why not go ahead and combine them, especially when they can taste so delicious?

Power

Losing weight with protein drinks

Week

You can lose a pound a day by stimulating the fat burning process with exercise, protein, and vital nutrients. The lack of these three elements is the sole reason why so many people today are overweight. No diet can help you achieve long-term weight loss. On the contrary, if you starve yourself, your body will attack your muscles and consume the only organs that burn fat. But you can prevent this by running 30 minutes every day—easily, without stress and with a smile—and by consuming protein, which prevents your body from breaking down muscle mass. Protein is also responsible for fat being sucked out of the fat cells and burned. Especially when you're trying to lose weight, your body needs protein that it can invest in muscles and fat burning hormones, such as the growth hormone HGH that builds muscles and melts fat. Another important factor is vital nutrients. We would all have a higher fat metabolism if our diet contained enough vital nutrients. Vitamin C boosts fat combustion, but this is also true of vitamin B6, magnesium, iodine, chromium, and selenium.

HOW TO MELT AWAY THE FAT

Prepare: Buy a good pair of running shoes and a pulse monitor. Ask your doctor whether it's safe for you to run and diet.

Run: Run 30 minutes every morning and evening, keeping your pulse below 140.

Consume protein: Drink three fitness drinks per day. For suggestions, see the next page.

Drink: Drink three quarts of water each day. Tea and vegetable juices are also permitted, but don't drink alcohol.

Consider a supplement: Choose a good multivitamin-mineral preparation. This will stimulate fat metabolism, fill up empty stores, and prevent deficiencies.

Fill up on fruit: In addition to the fruit drinks, you can also feast on pure fruit—as much as you want and whatever you want. The best are the tropical fruits and whatever fruits are in season.

Maintain your weight: Once you've lost enough weight, continue to run 30 minutes every day. If you can maintain your weight for three to six months, you're home free!

PLAN FOR THE WEEK

Monday

* ✳ Strawberry-Pineapple Mix ✳ Melon Shake ✳ Tomato-Avocado Drink

Tuesday

* ✳ Papaya-Orange Shake ✳ Cherry-Buttermilk Drink ✳ Icy Cucumber-Dill Drink

Wednesday

* ✳ Mango-Coconut Drink ✳ Chocolate-Pear Shake ✳ Carrot-Herb Shake

Thursday

* ✳ Kiwi-Grapefruit Drink with Mint ✳ Apricot-Almond Shake ✳ Mango-Carrot Mix

Friday

* ✳ Apple-Elderberry Drink ✳ Citrus-Buttermilk Flip ✳ Spicy Vegetable Shake

Saturday

* ✳ Berry Smoothie ✳ Banana-Yogurt Drink ✳ Kiwi-Avocado Mix

Sunday

* ✳ Peach Melba Cocktail ✳ C-Packed Blueberry Shake ✳ Celery Root Spinach Flip

Six reasons why it's worth switching on the blender

1. Protein power: Your protein tanks are empty. Replenish your stores with fitness drinks.

2. Fat burning power: Fitness drinks supply all the vital nutrients with few calories.

3: Muscle power: Protein prevents your body from taking away from your immune system to build up your muscles.

4. Brain doping: It's best to fill up your empty nutrient stores in the morning. Your brain will then have an ample supply to support serenity, creativity, and flashes of genius.

5. Cell rejuvenation: Our drinks contain all the nutrients your 70 billion cells need to renew themselves again and again.

6: Good mood material: Protein and nutrients from fruit or vegetables provide the basis for the happy messengers. Your body starts producing more serotonin and endorphins.

Seasonal Calendar
Fruits with enzymes are best
# of Fruit

IN PRAISE OF FRUIT

Do you eat fruit five times a day? If you answered no, you should start doing so now. Nothing provides you with more vital nutrients and healthy energy than fresh fruit from the Garden of Eden.

Fruit nourishes your thoughts because its fructose provides steady reinforcements for the brain without putting stress on your blood sugar level. Vital nutrients in fruit help to prevent fatigue, sharpen your concentration, and raise your spirits through the production of hormones.

Fruit keeps you thin. Its vitamin C, minerals, and phytochemicals boost fat metabolism and clean out the body by way of the kidneys. Fruit's fiber sets sluggish digestion in motion and carries toxins out of the intestines.

Fruit is medicine and has been used as such for millennia. Its vital nutrients strengthen your organs, aid in blood production, steady your nerves, and keep your digestive glands up and running. Fruit helps lower your blood pressure and keep your blood fat values low. It fortifies your immune system, purifies your intestines, cleans out all your blood vessels, and strengthens connective tissue in your skin and blood vessels. Fruit protects you against cancer, heart attacks, and strokes, mitigates asthma symptoms, and slows down the aging process. It helps you fall asleep and works against migraines. It strengthens your bones, raises your libido, and makes your hair shine. One thing's for certain: There's a fruit for every complaint; you just have to pluck it five times a day.

A tip for fitness and eternal youth: Every day, make yourself a large bowl of fruit salad using whatever fruits are in season.

Seasonal Calendar

	Jan	Feb	March	April	May	June	July	Aug	Sept	Oct	Nov	Dec
Apples	✳	✳	✳	✳	✳	✳	✳	✳	✳	✳	✳	✳
Apricots					✳	✳	✳	✳	✳			
Avocados	✳	✳	✳	✳	✳	✳	✳	✳	✳	✳	✳	✳
Bananas	✳	✳	✳	✳	✳	✳	✳	✳	✳	✳	✳	✳
Blackberries						✳	✳	✳	✳	✳		
Blueberries						✳	✳	✳	✳			
Cherries					✳	✳	✳	✳				
Currants						✳	✳	✳				
Dates	✳	✳	✳	✳	✳	✳	✳	✳	✳	✳	✳	✳
Elderberries									✳	✳	✳	
Figs (fresh)	✳	✳	✳	✳	✳	✳	✳	✳	✳	✳	✳	✳
Gooseberries					✳	✳	✳	✳				
Grapefruit	✳	✳	✳	✳	✳	✳	✳	✳	✳	✳	✳	✳
Grapes	✳	✳					✳	✳	✳	✳	✳	✳
Kiwis	✳	✳	✳	✳	✳	✳	✳	✳	✳	✳	✳	✳
Mangos	✳	✳	✳	✳	✳	✳	✳	✳	✳	✳	✳	✳
Melon	✳	✳	✳	✳	✳	✳	✳	✳	✳	✳	✳	✳
Oranges	✳	✳	✳	✳	✳	✳	✳	✳	✳	✳	✳	✳
Papaya	✳	✳	✳	✳	✳	✳	✳	✳	✳	✳	✳	✳
Peaches	✳	✳	✳	✳	✳	✳	✳	✳	✳			
Pears	✳	✳	✳	✳	✳	✳	✳	✳	✳	✳	✳	✳
Pineapple	✳	✳	✳	✳	✳	✳	✳	✳	✳	✳	✳	✳
Plums	✳	✳	✳	✳	✳	✳	✳	✳	✳	✳		
Raspberries						✳	✳	✳	✳			
Strawberries	✳	✳	✳	✳	✳	✳	✳	✳			✳	✳
Tangerines	✳	✳	✳							✳	✳	✳

✳ These dots indicate the months when the fruit is available.

✳ These dots indicate the high season for each fruit.

Berry
Soothing fitness drink
Smoothie

Rinse the berries briefly. Remove the stems from the berries and put them in a blender. Add the maple syrup and orange juice and blend thoroughly for fifteen seconds.

Cut the frozen banana into several pieces. Add the banana, protein powder, and water to the blender and blend vigorously for an additional fifteen seconds.

Pour the mixture into a frosted cocktail glass. Serve the drink with a straw.

Tip: To frost the cocktail glass, place it in the refrigerator or freezer for several hours ahead of time, or fill the glass with crushed ice and let it stand briefly.

Serves 1:

3 oz mixed berries
2 tsp maple syrup
2 tbs orange juice
1 medium banana, frozen
2 tbs protein powder
1/2 cup cold mineral water

 Berries

In Asia, these small spherical fruits are considered to be a folk remedy. They're jam-packed with vitamins and minerals. Berries' essential oils, pigments, and tannins fill you with energy, calm your nerves, and render you fit and relaxed. Their flavones protect you from cancer. In addition to boosting your metabolism, berries fortify your immune system, strengthen your heart, aid your kidneys in detoxifying your body, and help prevent rheumatism, arthritis, and diabetes.

Mango-Coconut
Tropical power for your cells
Drink

Peel and dice the mango. Set aside three nice mango cubes for garnish and place the remaining pieces in the blender.

Serves 1:
1 piece mango (about 4 oz)
1 lime
2 tsp brown sugar
1/4 cup cold unsweetened coconut milk
2 tbs protein powder
1/2 cup cold unfiltered apple juice
1-2 tbs grated coconut

Remove a spiral-shaped strip of zest from the lime and set it aside. Squeeze out the lime juice and add the lime juice, sugar, and coconut milk to the blender. Blend vigorously for fifteen seconds.

Add the protein powder and apple juice. Blend thoroughly for an additional ten seconds.

Moisten the rim of a large glass with water, turn the glass upside-down, and dip the rim into the grated coconut. Place ice cubes in the glass and pour the contents of the blender over the top. Thread the reserved mango cubes onto a cocktail skewer and lay them across the rim of the glass. Garnish with the lime zest. Serve the drink with a straw.

Coconut

This cannonball of minerals (mainly magnesium, iron, sodium, and selenium) protects your heart, calms your nerves, and maintains your stomach and intestines. This exotic fruit also supplies valuable plant protein. Coconut is the ideal fruit for combating stress. In Southeast Asia it's prescribed for heartburn and gastritis.

Strawberry-
The skinny drink
Pineapple Mix

Wash the strawberries and set aside one nice berry for garnish. Remove the stems from the remaining berries and cut them into quarters.

Serves 1:
3 oz strawberries
2 tsp lemon juice
1 tsp floral honey
2/3 cup cold pineapple juice
2 tbs protein powder

Put the strawberries, lemon juice, honey, and half of the pineapple juice in a blender and blend thoroughly for fifteen seconds.

Add the protein powder and the remaining juice and blend for an additional ten seconds.

Pour the mixture into a tall glass. Cut partway into the reserved strawberry and place it on the rim of the glass for garnish. Serve the drink with a straw.

Strawberries

Strawberries make you thin while you eat. These small red balls of fitness provide more fat burning vitamin C than lemons and have almost no calories: 4 ounces contain less than 40 calories. Strawberries' super fiber pectin lowers your cholesterol level and another 300 ingredients make them precious medicine. Strawberries aid digestion, clean mucous membranes, reduce fevers, serve as a diuretic, boost metabolism, and even send bacteria scurrying.

Papaya-Orange
Morning dose of fitness
Shake

Peel the papaya and remove the seeds. Cut away a nice wedge of papaya and set it aside for garnish. Dice the remaining papaya and place it in a blender. Add the lime juice, honey, and half of the orange juice and blend for fifteen seconds. Add the protein powder and the remaining orange juice and blend for an additional ten seconds. Place two ice cubes in a large glass and pour in the contents of the blender. Cut partway into the reserved papaya wedge and lime slice and place them on the rim of the glass. Serve the drink with a straw.

Serves 1:

4 oz ripe papaya

1 tbs lime juice

1 tsp floral honey

1/2 cup cold freshly squeezed orange juice

2 tbs protein powder

1 lime slice

Papaya

There are many reasons to start your day with papaya. It stimulates digestion and pampers your body with beta carotene, the nutrient that protects your cells against premature aging. Papaya's calcium and potassium content arm you against stress.

Kiwi-Grapefruit
Reinforce your immune system
Drink with Mint

Set aside one nice kiwi slice for garnish. Peel the remaining kiwi, dice it, and put it in a blender. Set aside one small mint sprig. Remove the remaining mint leaves from the stems and cut them into fine strips. Add the mint leaves, lemon juice, maple syrup, and half of the grapefruit juice to the blender. Blend thoroughly for fifteen seconds. Add the protein powder and the remaining juice and blend for an additional ten seconds.

Serves 1:
1 kiwi (about 4 oz)
2 small sprigs fresh mint
2 tsp lemon juice
2 tsp maple syrup
2/3 cup cold grapefruit juice
2 tbs protein powder

Place ice cubes in a large glass and pour the kiwi mixture over the top. Cut partway into the reserved kiwi slice and place it on the rim of the glass. Garnish with the reserved mint sprig. Serve the drink with a straw.

Kiwi

This exotic green fruit has three times the vitamin C of citrus fruit. It also contains the enzyme actinidin, which helps the digestive system break down protein. Kiwi also benefits your immune system (which is made up of 3 1/2 lb of protein). Combined with grapefruit, it provides your immune system with an extra dose of power.

Peach Melba Cocktail

A cool cup

Wash the raspberries, sort them, and set aside four or five nice berries for garnish. Put the remaining raspberries and 1 teaspoon of the maple syrup in a blender and purée the berries. Pour the berry purée into a large glass. Plunge the peach into a pot of boiling water for a few seconds to loosen the skin, then plunge it into a bowl of ice water. Remove the peach peel with a small knife. Cut the fruit in half, remove the pit, and cut the fruit into pieces. Put the peach, lemon juice, the remaining maple syrup, the protein powder, and half of the mineral water in the blender. Blend vigorously for fifteen seconds until the fruit is puréed.

Add the remaining mineral water and blend an additional ten seconds. Carefully pour the peach mixture over the puréed raspberries. Top with the frozen yogurt and garnish with the whole raspberries. Serve immediately with a spoon and fat straw.

Serves 1:
3 oz fresh raspberries
2 tsp maple syrup
1 ripe peach (about 4 oz)
2 tsp lemon juice
2 tbs protein powder
1/2 cup cold mineral water
1 scoop vanilla frozen yogurt

Peaches

With its abundance of aromatics, these sweet, juicy stone fruits woo every palate. Peaches also beguile your nerves with B vitamins, satisfy your immune system with vitamin C, and pamper your bones with a concentrated charge of calcium.

Kiwi-Avocado

Green fitness cocktail

Mix

Peel the avocado and chop the flesh, removing the pit. Put the avocado in a blender and drizzle with the lemon juice. Set aside one nice kiwi slice for garnish. Peel the remaining kiwi, chop it coarsely, and add it to the blender along with the sugar and half of the mineral water. Blend thoroughly for fifteen seconds. Add the protein powder and the remaining mineral water and blend thoroughly for an additional ten seconds.

Place ice cubes in a large glass and pour the avocado mixture over the top. Cut partway into the reserved kiwi slice and place on the rim of the glass. Garnish with the mint.

Serves 1:
2 oz ripe avocado
2 tbs lemon juice
1 kiwi (about 4 oz)
1 tsp brown sugar
1/2 cup cold mineral water
2 tbs protein powder
1 sprig fresh mint

Avocados

Avocados provide unsaturated fatty acids that are essential to health. They moisturize your skin, lubricate cell walls, and fortify your nerves. Along with the finest oil, they supply nutritious protein. Avocados' true magic is in their mannoheptulose, a unique carbohydrate that lowers the blood sugar level. Eating avocados will make you feel alive, focused, and alert. And the vitamin E in avocados will also protect your heart.

White

Joyfully refreshing

Fruit Cocktail

Peel the orange and lemon slices, and chop the fruit. Peel the apple quarter, remove the core, and cut the fruit into small pieces. Wash and dice the peach. Put the prepared fruit and half of the grape juice in a blender and blend thoroughly for fifteen seconds.

Add the protein powder, cinnamon, and the remaining juice and blend for an additional ten seconds.

Put ice cubes in a large glass and pour the fruit mixture over the top. Wash the grapes, remove the stems, thread them onto a small wooden skewer, and lay it across the rim of the glass. Serve the drink with a fat straw.

Serves 1:
1 orange slice
1 lemon slice
1/4 tart apple
1/4 peach
2/3 cup cold white grape juice
2 tbs protein powder
2 pinches ground cinnamon
3 small seedless grapes

Apples

Apples provide you with several hundred nutrients. They stimulate digestion, drive away bacteria, pep up your immune system, and keep you thin. Organic acids help your liver to detoxify and pectin lowers your cholesterol level, as well as protecting your intestines and blood vessels. Start off your day with an apple and end it with one too. Apples contain nutrients that wake you up in the morning and relax you at night.

Apple-Elderberry Drink

Sweet medicine

Wash the apple and set aside a nice wedge for garnish. Peel the remaining apple, remove the core, cut the fruit into small pieces, and put it in a blender.

Serves 1:
About 3 oz tart apple
2 tsp lemon juice
2 tsp floral honey
1/3 cup cold unfiltered apple juice
2 tbs protein powder
1/4 cup cold elderberry juice (natural foods store)
1 sprig fresh mint

Add the lemon juice, honey and apple juice to the blender and blend the contents thoroughly for fifteen seconds.

Add the protein powder and elderberry juice and blend vigorously for an additional ten seconds. Place ice cubes in a large glass and pour the mixture over the top. Place the apple wedge on the rim of the glass. Garnish the drink with mint and serve with a straw.

Elderberries

Elderberries contain the trace element selenium, which gives you a joyful serenity, protects all your cells, and counteracts heavy metals. In addition, elderberry juice is better for colds than the popular hot lemon.

Persimmon-

An autumn cocktail

Orange Drink

Serves 1:

**1/2 fully ripe Hachiya
persimmon (about 4 oz)**

1 tbs lime juice

2 tsp apple juice concentrate

1 tsp vanilla extract

**2/3 cup freshly squeezed
orange juice**

2 tbs protein powder

1 tiny sprig fresh mint

Wash the persimmon, cut it in half, and set aside a nice wedge for garnish. Peel the remaining persimmon, remove the core, and chop the fruit. Put the persimmon, lime juice, and apple juice concentrate in a blender. Add the vanilla extract and half of the orange juice. Blend the mixture thoroughly for fifteen seconds.

Add the protein powder and the remaining juice and blend for an additional ten seconds. Pour the mixture into a large glass. Cut partway into the persimmon wedge and place it on the rim of the glass. Garnish the drink with mint and serve with a straw.

Persimmons

These fist-sized, sweet, orange berries taste like a cross between a tomato and an apricot. They're the ideal brain food. Each contains up to 20 percent glucose, an instant burst of energy for the brain. Like all tropical fruits, persimmons are chockfull of vitamins and are especially rich in skin-protecting vitamin A.

Black Currant-

Power for your nerves

Banana Shake

Peel the banana. Cut out a diagonal slice and set it aside for garnish.
Chop the remaining banana coarsely and put it in a blender along
with the lemon juice, honey, and half of the juice.
Blend thoroughly for fifteen seconds.
Add the protein powder and the remaining juice
and blend for an additional ten seconds.
Put ice cubes in a tall glass and pour the mixture
over the top. Cut halfway into the banana slice and
place it on the rim of the glass. Serve the drink with
a straw.

Serves 1:
1/2 medium banana
1 tbs lemon juice
2 tsp floral honey
2/3 cup cold black currant juice
(natural foods store)
2 tbs protein powder

Black Currants

A single black currant supplies no less than two
milligrams of vitamin C. This power vitamin works
in every cell as a biological catalyst for countless
enzymatic processes, including in fat combustion, in
the immune system, and in the production of hard
connective tissue. It also gives you firm skin and
elastic blood vessels. Above all, during stressful times,
black currant juice steadies your nerves. And what
makes these sour berries even sweeter is that they
contain pantothenic acid, the vitamin that keeps
your hair from turning gray.

Melon Shake

A cocktail for your heart

Using a melon baller, remove five nice balls from the melon. Set aside the melon balls and a cut a wedge of melon for garnish. Peel the remaining melon, remove the seeds, cut the flesh into pieces, and put them in a blender. Rinse the mint and set aside a small sprig for garnish. Remove the remaining mint leaves, wash them, chop, and add them to the blender along with the apple juice concentrate and orange juice. Blend the contents thoroughly for fifteen seconds. Add the protein powder and milk and blend for an additional ten seconds.

Place ice cubes in a tall glass and pour the blender contents over the top. Thread the melon balls onto a cocktail skewer and lay them across the rim of the glass with the melon wedge. Garnish with the reserved mint sprig. Serve with a straw and a spoon.

Serves 1:
7 oz watermelon (or honeydew or galia melon)
2 sprigs fresh mint
1 tbs apple juice concentrate
2 tbs orange juice
2 tbs protein powder
2/3 cup cold low-fat milk

Melons

Everyone knows that, with only 12 calories per 4 oz, melons are the ideal slimming fruit. But what many people don't know is that melons are recommended by American cancer experts. This is because they contain large amounts of carotenoids. Melons support your kidneys, help prevent gout, and rheumatism and keep your blood thin. Researchers have found that melons contain adenosine, a chemical that acts like aspirin to prevent the clumping of blood platelets.

The beauty shake

Apricot-
Almond Shake

Wash the apricots, cut them in half, and remove the pits. Set aside a nice apricot wedge for garnish. Chop the remaining fruit coarsely and put it in a blender along with the apple juice concentrate, almond butter, and half of the milk. Blend vigorously for fifteen seconds. Add the remaining milk, protein powder, and vanilla extract. Blend briefly and vigorously.

Moisten the rim of a large glass with water, turn the glass upside-down, and dip the rim into the ground almonds.

Put ice cubes in the glass and pour the apricot mixture over the top. Cut partway into the reserved apricot wedge and place it on the rim of the glass. Serve the drink with a fat straw.

Serves 1:
2-3 fresh apricots
(about 2 1/2 oz)
1 tbs apple juice concentrate
2 tsp almond butter
(natural foods store)
2/3 cup cold low-fat milk
2 tbs protein powder
1 tsp vanilla extract
1-2 tbs ground almonds

Apricots

The Hunzas, a people in the Himalayas, live long lives. This could be because they eat so many apricots, a fruit with an especially high carotinoid content. Carotinoids are a plant pigment that renders free radicals harmless, thus protecting your blood vessels, heart, and brain. Apricots contain the beauty vitamin pantothenic acid. They give you vitality and boost fat degradation. Apricots' silicic acid strengthens connective tissue, meaning that it firms up your skin. They also provide large amounts of potassium, a natural diuretic.

Citrus-

Sweet and sour shake

Buttermilk Flip

Cut a nice slice from both the orange, and lemon and set them aside for garnish.

Peel the remaining orange, removing the white outer skin (pith). Cut the individual

orange segments from their membranes, collecting the

Serves 1:

1 orange

1 lemon

2 tbs freshly squeezed pink
grapefruit juice

1 egg yolk (optional)

1 tbs liquid fructose
(natural foods store)

1/2 cup cold buttermilk

2 tbs protein powder

dripping juice. Place the orange segments and juice in a

blender. Add the grapefruit juice, 1 tablespoon of the lemon

juice, the egg yolk (if using), fructose, and half of the

buttermilk. Blend the contents vigorously for fifteen seconds.

Add the protein powder, a little finely grated zest from the

lemon, and the remaining buttermilk and thoroughly blend for

an additional ten seconds. Pour the mixture into a large glass.

Cut partway into the reserved orange, and lemon slices and

place them on the rim of the glass. Serve the drink with a straw.

Citrus Fruits

We've all experienced the eye-opening
effects of vitamin C in the morning, in
the form of orange juice. But few of
us are aware that citrus's bioflavonoids
(especially in the white skin) intensify the
effects of the vitamin C. It's not necessary
to be so meticulous about peeling when
you eat citrus fruit.

Chocolate-Pear

Fruit for your sweet tooth

Shake

Heat the milk until lukewarm. Meanwhile, wash the pear. Cut away a nice wedge of the pear and set it aside for garnish. Peel the remaining pear, remove the core, cut the flesh into pieces, and put it in a blender. Add the orange juice, apple juice concentrate, chocolate (setting a little aside for garnish), and half of the milk. Blend thoroughly for fifteen seconds. Add the protein powder and the remaining milk and blend thoroughly for an additional ten seconds.

Pour the mixture into a tall glass and place the pear wedge on the rim. Sprinkle the drink with the remaining chocolate and serve with a straw.

Serves 1:
2/3 cup low-fat milk
About 4 oz ripe pear
1 tsp orange juice
1 tsp apple juice concentrate
2 tbs finely grated
unsweetened chocolate
2 tbs protein powder

Chocolate

Chocolate doesn't have to make you fat. If it's unsweetened chocolate and contains more than 60 percent cocoa, it doesn't affect insulin metabolism. Insulin, the fat storing hormone, stays locked away so that glucagon, the fat burning hormone, can break down the fat in the body. Interestingly cocoa beans supply more of the heart-protecting chemical polyphenol than a glass of red wine.

C-Packed
The drink of eternal youth
Blueberry Shake

Wash the fresh blueberries briefly, and pat dry or thaw the frozen

blueberries. Set aside ten nice berries for garnish. Place the remaining

berries, lemon juice, and kefir in a blender and blend

thoroughly for fifteen seconds.

Add the protein powder, ascorbic acid powder, and

milk and blend once more briefly and vigorously.

Pour the mixture into a tall glass. Thread the

reserved blueberries onto a cocktail skewer and lay

them across the rim of the glass. Serve the drink with

a fat straw.

Serves 1:
3 oz blueberries
(fresh or frozen)
1 tsp lemon juice
1/4 cup cold kefir
(natural foods store)
2 tbs protein powder
1 1/2 tsp ascorbic acid powder
1/2 cup cold low-fat milk

Blueberries

Blueberries are nature's lifestyle pills. They contain
an entire pharmacy of bioactive ingredients. They
help prevent cancer, fortify the immune system,
lower cholesterol and blood fat levels, and relieve
water retention. The tannins in blueberry skins
strengthen your intestines and their anthocyanin
(blue pigment) protects your cells, revitalizes
your body, and keeps you young. Blueberries are
the ideal accompaniment to kefir, the drink of
centenarians, supplemented by ascorbic acid
powder, pure vitamin C.

Cherry-Buttermilk

Purification cocktail

Drink

Wash the cherries and set aside a pair joined by their stems for garnish. Remove the pits from the remaining cherries and put the cherries in a blender. Remove the leaves from the mint and set aside one or two nice leaves. Chop the remaining mint leaves and add them to the blender along with the lemon juice, apple juice concentrate, protein powder, and half of the buttermilk. Blend thoroughly for fifteen seconds.

Serves 1:
4 oz sweet cherries
1 sprig fresh mint
1 tbs lemon juice
2 tsp apple juice concentrate
2 tbs protein powder
2/3 cup cold buttermilk

Add the remaining buttermilk and blend thoroughly for an additional ten seconds. Pour the mixture into a tall glass, hang the reserved cherries over the rim of the glass, and garnish with the reserved mint leaves.

Cherries

Their minerals (potassium, iron, and calcium), vitamins (C and folic acid) and plant pigments (anthocyanin) purify, detoxify, boost connective tissue formation, stimulate blood production, prevent inflammation, and strengthen the immune system and bones. Cherry therapy rejuvenates you while it softens and cleanses your skin.

Apple-Nut

For true happy hours

Shake

Toss 2 tablespoons of the hazelnuts in an ungreased skillet until they give off a toasted aroma. Remove the skillet from the heat. Wash the apple half and set aside a nice wedge for garnish. Peel the remaining apple, remove the core, chop the flesh, and put it in a blender. Add the lemon juice, cream, apple juice concentrate, and half of the milk and purée thoroughly for fifteen seconds.

Add the toasted hazelnuts, protein powder, and the remaining milk and blend for an additional ten seconds.

Brush a thin coating of honey onto the rim of a large glass and dip it into the remaining hazelnuts. Place ice cubes in the glass and fill with the apple-nut mixture. Serve with a straw.

Serves 1:
- 3 tbs finely grated hazelnuts
- 1/2 tart apple (about 4 oz)
- 1 tsp lemon juice
- 2 tbs cream
- 1 tbs apple juice concentrate
- 2/3 cup cold low-fat milk
- 2 tbs protein powder
- Honey

Nuts

Studies worldwide show that combining simple unsaturated fatty acids with the vitamin E in nuts protects your heart and circulation and slows down the aging of your cells, especially your brain cells. And munching nuts raises your spirits because nuts supply tryptophan, the material from which your body produces the youth hormone melatonin and the happy hormone serotonin. Nuts provide many minerals and salicylic acids, which prevent the clumping of blood platelets and thus help prevent strokes.

Banana-Yogurt Drink

Fit-for-fun cocktail

Peel the banana and set aside two slices for garnish. Coarsely chop the remaining banana and place it in a blender. Add the lemon juice, honey, yogurt, and half of the milk. Blend for fifteen seconds.

Add the protein powder and the remaining milk and blend vigorously for an additional ten seconds. Pour the drink into a tall glass. Thread the lemon slice and banana slices onto a cocktail skewer and place inside the glass. Serve the drink with a straw.

Serves 1:
1 large, ripe banana (about 4 oz)
1 tsp lemon juice
1 tbs floral honey
1/4 cup plain low-fat yogurt
1/2 cup cold low-fat milk
2 tbs protein powder
1 lemon slice

Bananas

Bananas make you merry. Four ounces supply 1.7 grams of serotonin. This important neurotransmitter makes you serene and resistant to stress and puts you in a good mood. It is a good fruit for people who lead high-stress lives because it soothes gastric complaints and fortifies mucous membranes. Eating something green before banana's valuable starch has been broken down into fructose and glucose helps process its nutrients.

Berry-Cherry

Steadies the nerves

Shake

Serves 1:
3 oz blackberries
2 tsp apple juice concentrate
1 tsp lemon juice
1/4 cup sour cherry juice
(natural foods store)
2 tbs protein powder
1/2 cup cottage cheese
2 tbs whipped cream

Wash and sort the blackberries. Set aside one blackberry for garnish. Put the remaining berries, apple juice concentrate, lemon juice, and cherry juice in a blender and blend thoroughly for 15 seconds. Press the fruit mixture through a fine sieve to remove the seeds.

Pour the fruit mixture back into the blender, and add the protein powder, and cottage cheese and blend vigorously for an additional ten seconds.

Place ice cubes in a large glass, pour the mixture over the top and garnish with whipped cream. Place the reserved blackberry on top. Serve the drink with a fat straw.

Blackberries

Blackberries supply loads of bioflavonoids, vitamins and minerals that keep you young, fortify your immune system, and arm your nerves against stress. These sweet, black, natural treasure chests contain, for example, carotenes, bioflavonoids, vitamin C, magnesium, and manganese.

Pineapple-
Lust for light
Kefir Drink

Remove the peel from the pineapple slice and set aside one piece of pineapple for garnish. Cut the remaining pineapple into small pieces, avoiding the core and put the fruit in a blender.

Squeeze the juice from the grapefruit and add the juice to the blender along with the sugar. Blend thoroughly.

Add the kefir and protein powder and blend at the lowest speed.

Place ice cubes in a tall glass and pour in the drink. Cut partway into the pineapple piece and place it on the rim of the glass. Serve the drink with a fat straw.

Serves 1:
1 thick slice of fresh pineapple
(about 4 oz with peel)
1/2 yellow grapefruit
2 tsp brown sugar
1/2 cup cold kefir
(natural foods store)
2 tbs protein powder

Pineapple

This exquisite tropical fruit is bursting with potassium, magnesium, phosphorus, iron, copper, zinc, manganese and iodine, all minerals that promote fat metabolism. The main contribution of pineapple to fitness is the enzyme bromelain, which aids in the digestion of protein. It guarantees that the important amino acids arrive at their place of effectiveness, your cells.

Weight-loss tip: Eat a slice of fresh pineapple before every meal.

Mango-
Carrot Mix

The drink of eternal youth, take two

Peel the mango. Cut away a nice mango wedge and set it aside for garnish. Coarsely chop the remaining mango and put it in a blender. Add the lime juice, honey, and half of the carrot juice and blend for fifteen seconds.

Add the remaining carrot juice, protein powder, and ginger and blend well for an additional ten seconds. Put ice cubes in a large glass and pour the mixture over the top. Place the mango wedge and carrot strips on the rim of the glass. Serve the drink with a straw.

Serves 1:
1 piece mango (about 4 oz)
1 tbs lime juice
2 tsp floral honey
2/3 cup cold carrot juice
2 tbs protein powder
2 pinches ground ginger
2 carrot strips (use a vegetable peeler)

Mangos

This fruit seduces you with its unique flavor and incomparable provitamin A content. With 6000 I.U. of vitamin A, mangos beat out every other fruit and any vitamin pill. Only carrots can keep up—and the two together are an ideal combination. Antiaging vitamin A prevents cancer and blocks free radicals, the destructive substances that cause your cells to age faster. Take care: Don't drink milk or alcohol two hours before or after eating mangos to avoid upsetting your stomach.

Tomato-Avocado Drink

A spicy revitalizer

Peel the avocado, dice the flesh, and put it in a blender. Drizzle with the lemon juice. Add half of the tomato juice and blend thoroughly for fifteen seconds.

Serves 1:
About 2 oz ripe avocado
2 tbs lemon juice
1/2 cup cold tomato juice
2 tbs protein powder
1/4 cup mineral water
Salt to taste
Pepper to taste
Several drops of Tabasco sauce
2 cherry tomatoes

Add the protein powder, the remaining tomato juice, and the mineral water. Season to taste with salt, pepper, and Tabasco. Blend vigorously for an additional ten seconds.

Put ice cubes in a glass and pour the mixture over the top. Wash the tomatoes, pat them dry, and use them to garnish the drink. Serve the drink with a straw.

Tomatoes

Doctors prescribe these "love apples" as an anticancer food (due to the lycopene), as a tonic for your heart and kidneys, and as a remedy for gout and rheumatism. Tomatoes are low in calories and their potassium content makes them a diuretic. They're rich in magnesium, calcium, iron, and zinc. Tomatoes' nutrients stimulate digestion, clean out your intestines, and keep you slim. And tomatoes improve your mood. A tomato drink in the morning makes you feel alive and optimistic and helps you deal with stress.

Spicy Vegetable Shake

Good mood mix

Wash and trim the bell pepper and tomatoes. Peel the celery root. Set aside a nice piece of bell pepper and celery root, and one cherry tomato for garnish. Dice the remaining vegetables. Rinse the parsley, set aside a small sprig for garnish, remove the remaining leaves from the stalks, and chop the leaves coarsely.

Put the bell pepper, celery root, tomatoes, and parsley in a blender. Add the tomato juice and blend thoroughly for fifteen seconds. Add the protein powder and stock, and season with herb salt and pepper. Blend vigorously for an additional ten seconds. Pour the drink into a tall glass. Thread the reserved bell pepper and celery root pieces and the cherry tomato onto a cocktail skewer and lay them across the rim of the glass. Garnish with the reserved parsley.

Serves 1:
2 oz red bell pepper
2-3 cherry tomatoes
2 oz celery root
3 sprigs fresh Italian parsley
1/2 cup cold spicy tomato juice
2 tbs protein powder
1/4 cup vegetable stock
Herb salt to taste
Black pepper to taste

Bell Peppers

Bell peppers are pure tonic. Their capsaicin and vitamin C fortify your immune system and their carotene (especially in red peppers) prevents cancer. Bell peppers aid digestion and circulation, work as a diuretic, ease pain, reduce stress, firm up connective tissue, improve concentration, and combat arthritis.

Icy Cucumber-
The fit and trim drink
Dill Drink

Dice the frozen cucumber and put it in a blender. Rinse the dill and set aside a nice sprig for garnish. Remove the remaining leaves from the stalks, chop the leaves coarsely, and add them to the blender along with the lemon juice, yogurt, and half of the kefir. Blend the contents thoroughly for fifteen seconds. Add the protein powder and the remaining kefir. Season with salt and pepper and blend thoroughly for an additional ten seconds.

Place ice cubes in a wide glass and pour the mixture over the top. Cut partway into the reserved cucumber slice and place it on the rim of the glass with the reserved dill. Serve the drink with a straw.

Serves 1:

1 piece frozen cucumber (about 3 oz, without peel or seeds)

3 small sprigs fresh dill

1 tsp lemon juice

1/4 cup plain low fat yogurt

1/2 cup cold kefir (natural foods store)

2 tbs protein powder

Salt to taste

Black pepper to taste

1 slice cucumber

Cucumbers

With only thirteen calories per 4 ounces and an insulin-like hormone, cucumbers are true fat burners. For their magnesium and potassium, cucumbers have been dubbed the fruit of athletes. Their juice drives water out of your body, making it easier on your heart. Cucumbers' bitter constituents stimulate the liver and gallbladder. Doctors prescribe cucumbers for gout and rheumatism as well as for cleansing the skin. A slice of cucumber on your skin can smooth wrinkles, soothe minor rashes, and relieve eczema.

Green temptation

Carrot-
Herb Shake

Wash the herbs and shake them dry. Set aside a small sprig of chervil for garnish. Remove the remaining chervil and parsley leaves from their stalks and chop the leaves finely. Put the herbs in a blender along with the lemon juice, honey, hazelnuts, and carrot juice. Blend vigorously for fifteen seconds. Add the protein powder and milk. Season with salt, pepper, Worcestershire sauce, and olive oil. Blend for an additional ten seconds.

Pour the drink into a tall glass. Lay the carrot stick across the rim of the glass and garnish the drink with the reserved chervil.

Serves 1:
1 handful fresh chervil
3 sprigs fresh Italian parsley
1 tbs lemon juice
1 tsp floral honey
2 tbs ground hazelnuts
1/4 cup cold carrot juice
2 tbs protein powder
1/2 cup cold low-fat milk
Salt to taste
Black pepper to taste
1-2 drops Worcestershire sauce
A couple drops of olive oil
1 carrot stick

Carrots

Due to their high pectin content (a fiber that promotes healthy intestines) and skin-protecting vitamin A, carrots are an essential ingredient in fitness cocktails. Tip: Always consume them with a little olive oil so that their vitamin A can be easily transported to your cells.

Beet Cream

Contributes to a long life

Serves 1:

4-5 radishes (about 2 oz)
2 tbs low-fat plain yogurt
1/4 cup beet juice
2 tsp lemon juice
1/2 tsp grated horseradish
2 tbs protein powder
1/2 cup cold buttermilk
Salt to taste
Black pepper to taste
1 tsp chopped fresh chives

Wash and trim the radishes. Cut two nice slices from the radishes and set them aside for garnish. Chop the remaining radishes and put them in a blender along with the yogurt, beet juice, lemon juice, and horseradish. Blend well for fifteen seconds.

Add the protein powder and buttermilk. Season generously with salt and pepper and blend thoroughly for an additional ten seconds.

Pour the mixture into a large glass. Cut partway into the radish slices and place them on the rim of the glass. Sprinkle with the chives. Serve the drink with a fat straw.

Beets

These antiaging vegetables provide two fountains of youth: Folic acid and silicium. Folic acid protects blood vessels and the heart and participates in the production of hormones such as dopamine and norepinephrine that promote good moods, creativity, and power. Silicium is the trace element for beauty. It fortifies connective tissue and gives you firm skin, shiny hair, and hard nails. In addition, beets detoxify your body, work as a diuretic, and promote cell growth and the formation of red blood cells.

Celery Root

The anti-stress shake

Spinach Flip

Peel the celery root and set aside a narrow wedge for garnish. Grate the remaining celery root. Wash the spinach thoroughly, trim it, and chop it coarsely. Rinse the parsley and set aside a small sprig for garnish. Remove the remaining parsley leaves from the stalks and chop the leaves. Put the celery root, spinach, and parsley in a blender. Add the egg yolk, if using, lemon juice, and celery juice. Blend well for fifteen seconds. Add the protein powder and milk. Season with salt, pepper, and nutmeg and blend thoroughly for an additional ten seconds.

Pour the mixture into a tall glass. Cut partway into the celery root wedge and place it on the rim of the glass. Grind a little pepper over the top and garnish with the reserved parsley. Serve with a straw.

Serves 1:

2 oz celery root

1 oz tender spinach leaves

3 sprigs fresh Italian parsley

1 egg yolk (optional)

2 tsp lemon juice

1/4 cup celery juice (natural foods store)

2 tbs protein powder

1/2 cup cold low-fat milk

Salt to taste

Black pepper to taste

1 pinch freshly ground nutmeg

Celery Root

This vegetable lowers stress-related high blood pressure. In Asia, celery root has been used for 2000 years as a blood pressure-reducing remedy. The active substance 3-N-butyl phthalide reduces the stress hormones in the blood that constrict blood vessels. Certainly Hippocrates wasn't yet aware of this, but he still recommended celery root for everyone "whose nerves flutter."

Tutti-Frutti
Nature's energy drink
Cocktail

Wash and trim or peel the fruit. Set aside several pieces for garnish. Cut the remaining fruit into small pieces and put them in a blender along with the lemon juice, fructose, cottage cheese, and half of the low-fat milk. Blend thoroughly for fifteen seconds.

Add the protein powder, oat flakes, and the remaining milk and blend well for an additional ten seconds. Put ice cubes in a large glass and pour the mixture over the top. Thread the reserved fruit onto a small cocktail skewer and lay it across the rim of the glass. Serve the drink with a fat straw.

Serves 1:
4 oz mixed fruit (e.g.,
strawberries, green grapes,
blackberries, bananas)
2 tsp lemon juice
1 tbs liquid fructose
(natural foods store)
2 tbs low-fat cottage cheese
1/2 cup cold low-fat milk
3 tbs protein powder
2 tbs instant oatmeal

 Grapes

Grapes contain boron, which strengthens bones and helps prevent osteoporosis. Their B vitamins steady your nerves, their folic acid stimulates blood production, their vitamin C feeds your immune system, their potassium lowers your blood pressure, and their magnesium fortifies your muscles and heart. Grapes keep your intestines and kidneys functioning and promote better concentration.

Mocha-Banana

With stimulating espresso

Dream

Put the espresso and sugar in a blender. Peel the banana, cut it into several pieces, and add them to the blender along with half of the milk. Blend thoroughly for ten seconds.

Add the protein powder and the remaining milk and blend vigorously for an additional ten seconds. Moisten the rim of a tall glass and dip it into the espresso powder. Place ice cubes in a tall glass and pour the mixture over the top. Garnish with the whipped cream and the remaining espresso powder. Serve the drink with a straw and a long-handled spoon.

Serves 1:

1/4 cup cold espresso
1 tsp brown sugar
2 oz banana
2/3 cup cold low-fat milk
3 tbs protein powder
1 tbs instant espresso powder
1 tbs whipped cream

Coffee

The components of coffee boost metabolisms and stimulate brain activity. Coffee drinkers read faster, have a better short-term memory, and have a 40 percent lower risk of gallstones than non-coffee drinkers. Caffeine not only expands minds but also expands constricted bronchial tubes (asthma). Researchers in Scotland found that heart disease is more common in people who don't drink coffee. A healthy dose: One to three cups per day.

Chocolate-

Gives feelings of love

Orange Shake

Gradually bring the milk to a boil. Chop the chocolate coarsely, add it to the milk, and melt it while stirring occasionally. Remove the chocolate milk from the heat, pour it into a heatproof measuring cup or pitcher, and refrigerate for thirty minutes.

Pour the cold chocolate milk into a blender. Add the lemon juice, protein powder, and vanilla extract and blend well for fifteen seconds.

Put the orange sherbet in a tall glass and pour the chocolate milk over the top. Cut partway into the orange slice and place it on the rim of the glass. Serve the drink with a long-handled spoon and a straw.

Serves 1:
1 cup low-fat milk
2 oz unsweetened chocolate
1 tsp lemon juice
3 tbs protein powder
1 tsp vanilla extract
1 scoop orange sherbet
1/2 slice orange

Vanilla

The black bean whose pulp lends desserts an incomparable flavor originated in Central America and is a member of the orchid family. The wives of Aztec rulers knew the effects of cocoa drinks seasoned with vanilla on their men. Vanilla stimulates the kidneys, fortifies the stomach, and promotes good digestion. Vanilla was once forbidden in cloisters.

Tangy
Lime Shake

Sour power

Wash the lime under hot water, dry it, and finely grate the zest. Cut the lime in half and squeeze the juice from both halves. Put the lime juice, lime zest, cream cheese, and cream in a blender. Add the sugar and half of the milk and blend vigorously for fifteen seconds.

Add the protein powder and the remaining milk and thoroughly blend for an additional ten seconds.

Pour the mixture into a large glass. Cut partway into the strawberry and place it on the rim of the glass. Garnish the drink with the lime zest strip and serve it with a fat straw.

Serves 1:

1 lime (or 1/2 lemon)

1/3 cup low-fat cream cheese

2 tbs cream

2 tsp brown sugar

1/2 cup cold low-fat milk

3 tbs protein powder

1 ripe firm strawberry

1 strip of lime zest

Lime

Although this "lemon of the tropics" has less vitamin C than its big sister the lemon, it provides other benefits. It is rich in potassium, calcium, phosphorus, and aromatic oils. And it cheers the organic heart because its rind is usually untreated, allowing you to grate it and use its healthy bitter constituents as a spice.

Raspberry-Poppy Seed Cream

Sweet, irresistible seduction

In a saucepan, bring the milk and cream to a boil. Slit open the vanilla bean lengthwise, scrape out the pulp and add the bean and pulp to the milk. Sprinkle in two-thirds of the poppy seeds and simmer for five minutes over very low heat. Remove the vanilla bean.

Serves 1:
1/2 cup cold low-fat milk
2 tbs cream
1/2 vanilla bean
1 tbs poppy seeds
3 oz raspberries
1 tbs maple syrup
3 tsp lemon juice
3 tbs protein powder
1 lemon slice

Briefly rinse the raspberries and sort them. Set aside four nice berries for garnish. Put the remaining raspberries, maple syrup, two teaspoons of the lemon juice, and six tablespoons of the poppy seed milk in the blender and blend for fifteen seconds. Add the protein powder and the remaining poppy seed milk and blend for an additional ten seconds. Moisten the rim of a glass with the remaining lemon juice and dip it into the remaining poppy seeds. Pour the milk mixture into the glass.

Thread the lemon slice and reserved raspberries onto a cocktail skewer and lay them across the rim of the glass. Serve the drink with a straw.

Raspberries

In France, raspberries are considered to be a medicinal plant. They spice up your health with potassium (to reduce blood pressure), iron (to promote blood production), and magnesium (to fortify heart and muscles). Their acids, pectin, and tannins aid the liver in detoxifying the body and even reduce fevers. Raspberries' biotin adds shine to your hair, their seeds stimulate digestion, and their carotenes protect your skin and sharpen your vision.

Index

> **Abbreviations**
> tsp = teaspoon
> tbs = tablespoon

Credits

Published originally under the title
FOREVER YOUNG: Fitneß-Drinks
plus Eiweiß
© 2000 Gräfe und Unzer Verlag
GmbH, Munich

English translation copyright for
the US edition © 2001 Silverback
Books, Inc.

Project editor: Lisa M. Tooker
Editors: Marion Grillparzer, Jennifer
Newens, CCP
Reader: Maryna Zimdars
Cover design: independent Medien-
Design, Claudia Fillmann
Inside layout: Heinz Kraxenberger
Production: Helmut Giersberg,
Patty Holden
Recipes: Martina Kittler
Photos: Matteo Manduzio
Also: StockFood Eising: pp. 5, 10, 16,
17, 22, 27, 32, 34, 36, 40, 41, 50, 58, 61
Food styling: Olivia Benini-Lazzerone
Typesetting: Johannes Kojer
Reproduction: Repro Schmidt,
Dornbirn
Printing: Appl, Wemding
Binding: Sellier, Freising

ISBN: 1-930603-31-2
Printed in Hong Kong through
Global Interprint,
Santa Rosa, California

Dr. Ulrich Strunz studied nuclear physics and medicine in Germany and abroad. He has performed research and published various works on the hormonal control of bodily functions (almost 100 scientific publications). He is currently a practicing internist and orthomo-lecular doctor and a personal physician to competitive and non-competitive athletes. At the age of 45, Strunz started participating in extreme sports and is now a world-class, ultra-triathlete in his age group.

Dr. Strunz holds fitness seminars and also writes books on the subject.

Caution
The techniques and recipes in this book are to be used at the reader's sole discretion and risk. Always consult a doctor before beginning a new eating plan.

SILVERBACK

BOOKS, INC.